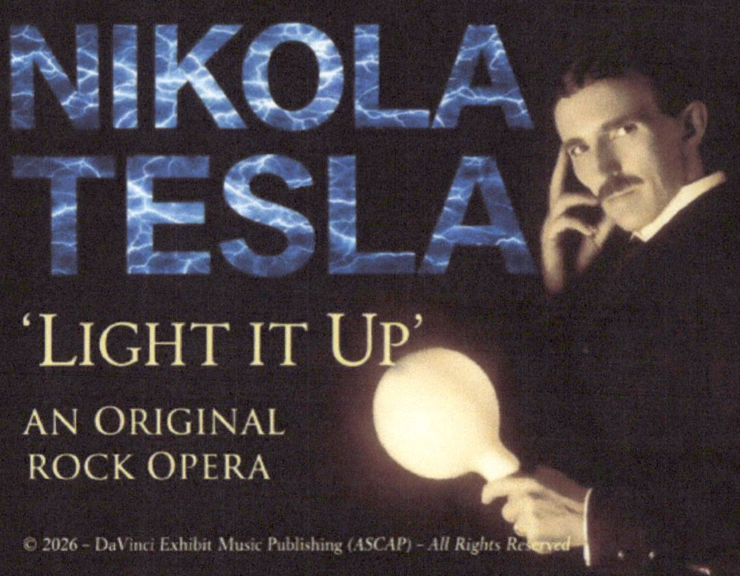

Nikola Tesla was one of the greatest visionaries in human history, a creative genius who shaped the electrical age, powered the modern world, and imagined a future far beyond his time. That vision, that obsession, that humanity, that legacy – now electrified for the stage!

Nikola Tesla
'Light It Up'
An Original Rock Opera
Written by: Rodgers and Rodgers
World Premiere

June 20, 2026 – Delmar Hall - St. Louis, MO

Very Special Thanks
Mary Catherine McDonough – Maria Rodgers O'Rourke
Frank Chiocchi – Paul R. Friedman – Ali, Caitlin, and Tierney

contact@teslalightitup.com
Phone: +01 720 504 9408
www.teslalightitup.com

Nikola Tesla "Light It Up" An Original Rock Opera

Songs in Order of Appearance

1 Born Tesla (3:32)

2 Light It Up – The Beginning (Reprise) (4:44)

3 Money and Imagination (2:20)

4 Dinner at Delmonico's (4:58)

5 I am the Original Wizard of OZ (4:21)

6 Hiding Inside My Mind (3:09)

7 Colorado Cosmic Cowboy (3:28)

8 Wardenclyffe (5:12)

9 Liars, Thieves, Knaves, Highwaymen, and Banditos' (3:04)

10 Presence (5:32)

11 Standing On My Grave (3:42)

12 Peace (4:52)

13 Light It Up (Main Theme) (3:36)

BORN TESLA

Written by Rodgers and Rodgers

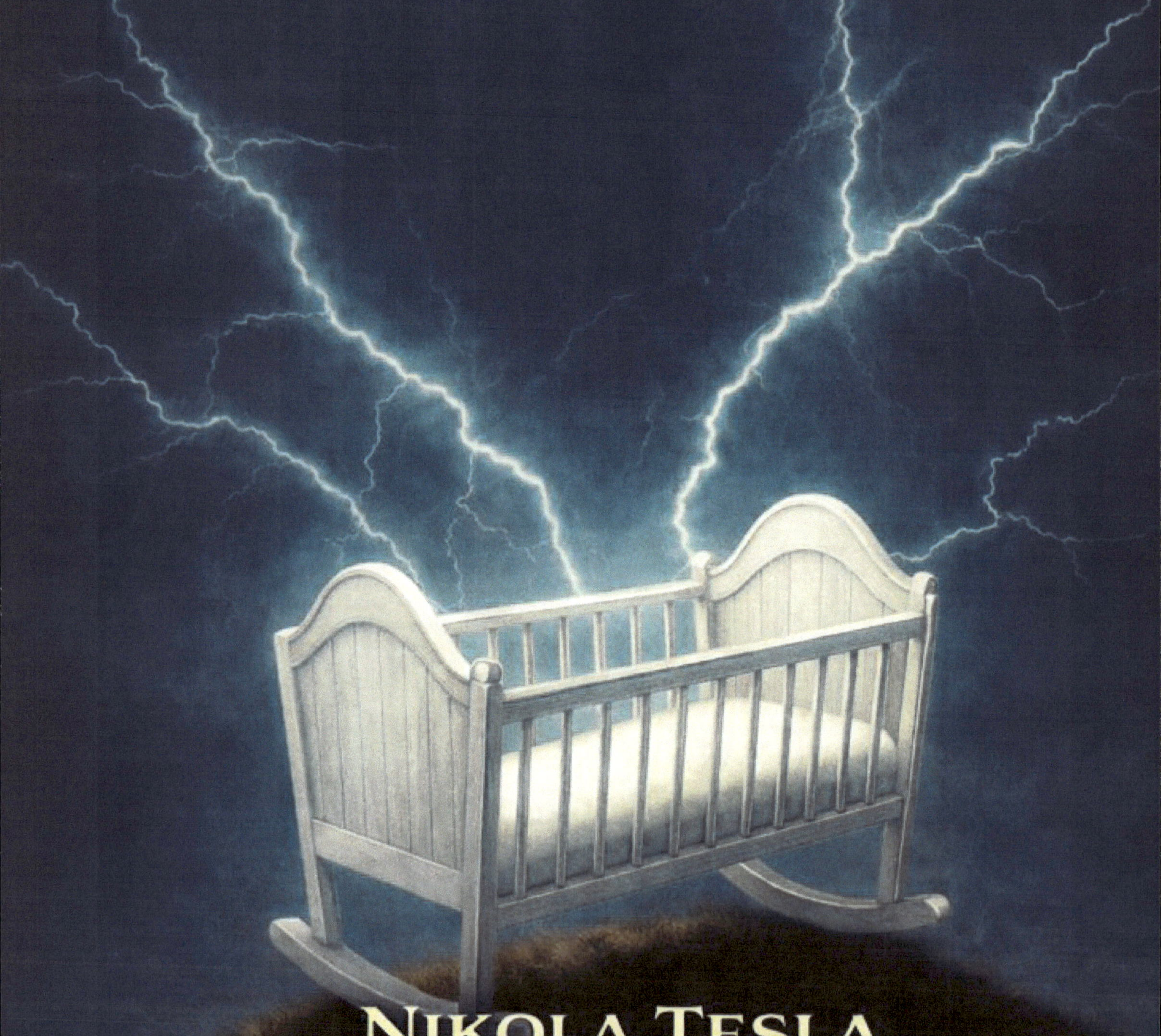

NIKOLA TESLA

"LIGHT IT UP"

AN ORIGINAL ROCK OPERA

Born at midnight, through a thundering tempest,
A "child of the storm", the midwife cried,
"Oh no, he will be known as a child of light", I replied.

In the routine of performing the mechanics of living,
I'm apt to forget the inner child at my side,
Steppingstones, a guide, a path I must give him,
To help him along his way in life.

The ordinary will become the extraordinary,
His reach will now exceed his grasp,
The hand that rocked the cradle,
Will rule the world..... at last!

I must teach him to be kind, good, and honest,
To help his fellow human beings,
His greatest critic, a self-accounting to himself,
To rely on his own judgement for everything.

When he lingers for a moment too long,
Or pauses for more than an instant,
He'll remember how he got to there from here,
Unrelenting love, patience, practice, and commitment.

The ordinary will become the extraordinary,
His reach will now exceed his grasp,
The hand that rocked the cradle,
Will rule the world.... at last!

The ordinary will become the extraordinary,
His reach will now exceed his grasp,
The hand that rocked the cradle,
Will rule the world.... at last!

• "Born Tesla" is the opera's mythic genesis song — the moment where destiny, motherhood, prophecy, and invention converge in one storm-lit birth scene that establishes the spiritual foundation of Tesla's entire life.

• The song opens in Smiljan on the night of Tesla's birth, during a violent lightning storm, placing his arrival in direct communion with the elemental force that will define his future: electricity itself.

• The thunderstorm is not merely a meteorological setting — it functions as cosmic foreshadowing, suggesting that nature itself is heralding the arrival of a child whose life will one day master lightning.

• The midwife's fearful declaration that the newborn is "a child of the storm" reflects superstition, dread, and the belief that such violent conditions foretell chaos or destruction.

• Đuka Tesla's response — "No, he will be known as a child of light" — is one of the opera's defining prophetic moments, transforming fear into revelation and recasting the storm as a sign not of darkness, but illumination.

• This line establishes light as the central symbolic thread of the entire rock opera: light as invention, enlightenment, transcendence, and humanity's future.

• Georgina "Đuka" Tesla is portrayed not simply as mother, but as prophet, architect, and first visionary of Tesla's destiny — the one person who recognizes, from the beginning, the magnitude of what has entered the world.

• Her calm presence amid the storm reflects her historical character: a woman of profound intelligence, strength, discipline, and inner creativity, grounded enough to remain unshaken where others panic.

• Though never formally educated, Đuka possessed extraordinary memory and inventive talent, designing practical mechanical devices in daily life — a trait Tesla himself later credited as the origin of his own genius.

• Tesla often said his ability to mentally construct inventions in complete detail before building them came directly from his mother, making her not only his parent, but the genetic and spiritual source of his imaginative process.

• The lyric "In the routine of performing the mechanics of living, I'm apt to forget the inner child at my side" beautifully humanizes Đuka, showing her awareness that motherhood is both practical labor and sacred guardianship.

• Here, she is not simply raising a son — she is shaping a future force whose gifts must be guided with patience and moral clarity.

• "Steppingstones, a guide, a path I must give him" reveals her conscious sense of responsibility: she understands that genius alone is insufficient without character, discipline, and ethical direction.

• The chorus line "The ordinary will become the extraordinary" is central to the meaning of the song: it expresses the miraculous transformation from fragile infant to world-changing visionary, suggesting that greatness begins in the most humble human beginnings.

• **This line also reflects a universal truth embedded in Tesla's story** — that genius is born in ordinary places, under ordinary conditions, and becomes extraordinary through vision, nurture, and relentless devotion.

• "His reach will now exceed his grasp" is profoundly layered: it implies that Tesla's ambitions will extend beyond existing human limits, beyond what even seems possible to contain or control.

- The phrase evokes both aspiration and destiny — Tesla's mind will always reach farther than the world is ready to follow, making his life one of perpetual transcendence beyond accepted boundaries.

- It also hints at the paradox of genius: to exceed one's grasp is both triumph and burden, because vision often outruns the means to realize it fully in one lifetime.

- **The line "The hand that rocked the cradle will rule the world at last" is among the opera's most emotionally powerful metaphors.**

- **In the song's deepest interpretation, Đuka is referring not merely to her son, but to herself: her own unrealized dreams for invention and service to humanity will now live through Nikola.**

- **The phrase becomes an act of spiritual inheritance** — she recognizes that what she could imagine but never fully bring into the world herself will now be incarnated in him.

- Thus, Tesla becomes the vessel of his mother's unrealized genius: her dreams, intellect, and longing to help humanity are reborn through her son's future achievements.

- "I must teach him to be kind, good, and honest" grounds the prophetic grandeur of the song in moral urgency: Đuka understands that genius without humanity is dangerous, and that ethical character must equal intellectual power.

- Her insistence that he "help his fellow human beings" reveals the opera's moral framing of Tesla's mission — invention is not for fame or wealth, but for service to mankind.

- "His greatest critic, a self-accounting to himself" captures Tesla's lifelong perfectionism and relentless inner discipline, traits that would define both his brilliance and his suffering.

- The line suggests that from earliest childhood, Tesla is being shaped not for external approval, but for inner standards so exacting they become both strength and torment.

- "To rely on his own judgement for everything" foreshadows Tesla's independence of mind — the fierce self-reliance that would allow him to challenge accepted science, yet also isolate him from collaborators and institutions.

- **The lyric about lingering too long and remembering "how he got to there from here" reflects the discipline of persistence: Tesla's path will not be built on luck, but on patience, love, and relentless practice.**

- **"Unrelenting love, patience, practice, and commitment" becomes Đuka's formula for genius — a maternal creed that balances inspiration with discipline.**

- Dramatically, this song is essential because it establishes Tesla's destiny not as accident, but as inheritance: his genius is born from lineage, prophecy, and the shaping hand of a mother who sees farther than anyone else.

- Musically, "Born Tesla" functions as the opera's sacred overture into narrative — its emotional tone should feel reverent, storm-charged, and deeply maternal, balancing intimacy with cosmic grandeur.

- **In the larger arc of the opera, this song plants every major theme that follows: light versus darkness, invention as destiny, sacrifice for humanity, and the cost of visionary reach.**

- "Born Tesla" ultimately becomes more than a birth song — it is the annunciation of a prophet of electricity, and the declaration that behind every great visionary stands an unseen force who first believed in the light before the world could see it.

- Additional Song Inspiration by Mary Catherine McDonough Rodgers

NIKOLA TESLA

'LIGHT IT UP'

(Reprise)

The Beginning

Written by Rodgers and Rodgers
© 2026 ASCAP

I'd wave my hands in front of my eyes,
To see what was real or if my mind was adrift,
What I thought was an affliction,
Turned out to be a gift.

Sensing the power of visualization,
Illuminating flashes were no hallucinations,
Only a receiver to the great unknown,
A celestial connection on a cosmic phone.
Oooooooh, Oooooooh, Oooooooh

Cosmic Communications,
Energy, frequency, and vibrations,
Power, pulsating from pole to pole,
I feel the world's electrical soul,
Exclaim to Erebus .... enoughs, enough,
From now to forever ..... Let's Light It Up!

Dream, imagine, create, and wonder,
Are all in the public domain,
An unlimited repertoire,
Plays in my brain.

Harnessing the sun can't be that tough,
I just haven't thought.... hard enough.
I can feel the presence of the powers that be,
Mount Olympus is contacting me.
Cosmic Communications,
Energy, Frequency, and Vibrations,
Power, pulsating from pole to pole,
I feel the world's electrical soul,
Exclaim to Erebus .... enoughs, enough,
From now to forever ..... Let's Light It Up!

You can't do that, because it can't be done,
The fools would say,
Those who will come to scoff will remain to pray.

Cosmic Communications
Energy, frequency, and vibrations,
Power, pulsating from pole to pole
I feel the world's electrical soul,
Exclaim to Erebus .... enoughs, enough,
From now to forever ..... Let's Light It Up!

• "Light It Up (The Beginning) – Reprise" is the spiritual invocation of the rock opera — the quiet awakening before the electrical storm, where Tesla first steps forward not as public legend, but as a solitary consciousness revealing the inner source of his genius.

• Positioned immediately after "Born Tesla," this reprise serves as the opera's first true self-portrait of Tesla as an adult: the audience has witnessed his prophetic birth, and now they are invited inside his mind for the first time.

• Unlike the full anthem version of "Light It Up," which is triumphant and declarative, this reprise is contemplative, intimate, and searching — less proclamation than confession.

• The slow piano arrangement is dramatically essential because it creates emotional contrast: instead of explosive spectacle, the audience encounters Tesla in stillness, hearing the private thoughts that precede his public greatness.

• This song functions as Tesla's internal monologue — a man standing alone before the world, thinking aloud, trying to explain sensations and perceptions that no ordinary person could fully understand.

• The opening lines, "I'd wave my hands in front of my eyes, to see what was real or if my mind was adrift," immediately establish vulnerability: Tesla is describing not triumph, but childhood uncertainty, when his extraordinary visions felt frightening and disorienting.

• In this quieter context, the lyric becomes even more poignant than in the anthem version — it feels less like revelation and more like memory revisited with humility and wonder.

• "What I thought was an affliction turned out to be a gift" becomes the emotional hinge of the reprise: the audience hears Tesla recognizing that the very thing that isolated him from others became the source of everything he would give humanity.

• Here, that line carries tenderness rather than triumph — it is gratitude born from hard-won understanding.

• "Sensing the power of visualization" introduces the audience to Tesla's most extraordinary faculty: his ability to see inventions fully formed in the theater of his mind before they existed physically.

• "Illuminating flashes were no hallucinations" is especially moving in this stripped-down arrangement because it reframes what once frightened him as sacred signals — not symptoms of madness, but transmissions of genius.

• The phrase "Only a receiver to the great unknown" is the theological center of Tesla's identity: he does not experience himself as creator in isolation, but as an instrument tuned to receive truths from a greater universal intelligence.

• "A celestial connection on a cosmic phone" remains one of the opera's most brilliant metaphors, but in this reprise it becomes deeply personal — not exuberant cosmic swagger, but quiet astonishment that such communication is even possible.

• The wordless "Ooooooh" passage is dramatically powerful because it allows the audience to dwell in Tesla's sense of awe — a suspended moment where emotion exceeds language.

• It gives musical voice to what cannot be explained rationally: wonder, mystery, and the sacred strangeness of receiving ideas from beyond ordinary perception.

• "Cosmic Communications, Energy, Frequency, and Vibrations" functions here almost like prayer or incantation — Tesla is naming the elemental laws through which he understands the universe.

• In the reprise, these words feel meditative rather than declarative, as if Tesla is grounding himself in the invisible principles that govern both his inventions and his inner life.

• "Power, pulsating from pole to pole, I feel the world's electrical soul" is especially profound in this version because it is experiential rather than triumphant: Tesla is not announcing mastery, he is describing sensation — the visceral awareness that he can feel the living current of the planet itself.

• The invocation to Erebus retains all its mythic force here, but its dramatic tone shifts from battle cry to solemn declaration.

• Erebus, primordial embodiment of darkness born from Chaos, symbolizes not only literal darkness but ignorance, fear, and the unawakened state of human civilization.

• "Exclaim to Erebus… enough's enough" becomes, in this quieter version, a deeply personal vow: Tesla is not yet commanding the world, but privately declaring that darkness — in himself and in civilization — must end.

• "From now to forever… Let's Light It Up!" in the reprise feels less like a crowd anthem and more like the moment Tesla first commits inwardly to his lifelong mission of illumination.

• It is the seed before the full flowering of the anthem: the private oath that precedes the public proclamation.

• "Dream, imagine, create, and wonder are all in the public domain" is especially meaningful this early in the opera because it establishes Tesla's philosophy before the world knows his achievements.

• It reveals that even before fame, his worldview is rooted in radical generosity — imagination belongs to humanity, not ownership.

• "An unlimited repertoire plays in my brain" becomes more poignant here because it carries loneliness as well as wonder: Tesla's mind is endlessly fertile, but also crowded with thoughts few others can understand.

• "Harnessing the sun can't be that tough, I just haven't thought hard enough" reveals Tesla's quiet audacity with understated elegance — in this reflective setting, it sounds less boastful and more like the natural thought process of a man for whom impossibility simply does not exist.

• "I can feel the presence of the powers that be, Mount Olympus is contacting me" in this version sounds less theatrical and more mystical — as though Tesla is describing an authentic, almost sacred sensation of communion with higher intelligence.

• Mount Olympus here becomes symbolic not of literal gods, but of transcendent knowledge — Tesla sensing himself in contact with the archetypal realm of cosmic design.

• The bridge lyric "You can't do that, because it can't be done, the fools would say" gains extraordinary dramatic weight in this reprise because it arrives before Tesla's triumphs, making it prophetic rather than retrospective.

• Here, it is not a victory lap over doubters — it is Tesla foreseeing resistance before it comes, already aware that the world will challenge what it cannot imagine.

• "Those who will come to scoff will remain to pray" is transformed into prophecy: Tesla is predicting the inevitable reversal when disbelief collapses into awe.

• This gives the reprise a powerful dramatic tension — the audience knows they are hearing the calm certainty of a man already aware of the battles ahead.

• Structurally, this song is the calm before the storm because it creates a sacred pause in the opera's architecture: after the mythic birth of "Born Tesla," it gives the audience inward access before the spectacle and conflict begin.

• It is the moment where Tesla first stands fully before us not as symbol, myth, or child of prophecy, but as conscious visionary — self-aware, searching, and already connected to forces larger than himself.

• Musically, the piano arrangement feels spacious, reverent, and emotionally transparent, allowing breath and silence to become part of the storytelling.

• In contrast to the anthem version's expansive triumph, this reprise is an intimate revelation: the anthem is Tesla proclaiming his mission to the world; the reprise is Tesla whispering that mission first to himself.

• Thematically, it establishes the opera's entire emotional contract with the audience: that what follows is not merely the story of inventions, but the unfolding journey of a mind in communion with light itself.

• "Light It Up (The Beginning) – Reprise" becomes the sacred ignition spark of the opera — the first quiet current before the voltage rises, the private awakening before the world is illuminated forever.

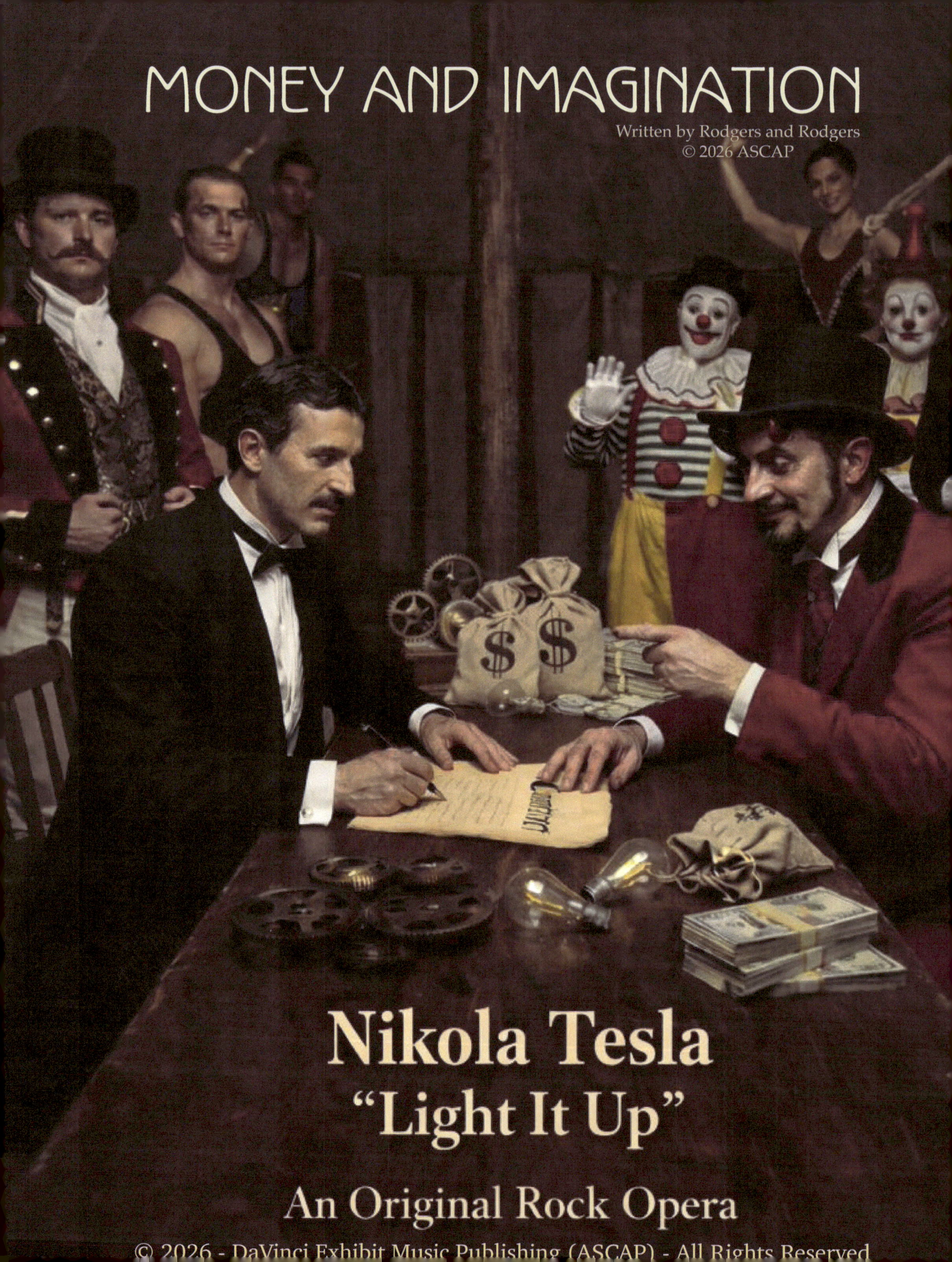
MONEY AND IMAGINATION
Written by Rodgers and Rodgers
© 2026 ASCAP
Nikola Tesla
"Light It Up"
An Original Rock Opera
© 2026 - DaVinci Exhibit Music Publishing (ASCAP) - All Rights Reserved

I can believe I'm even talking to this guy,
What a jerk, what a pompous ass,
He thinks he knows everything about everything,
If you don't believe him, just ask.

He fumbles through his theories, never sure what fits,
He'll steal my ideas in a second and claim,
"Hey, it's just biz!"
Why is this guy even talking to me? Oh, I know why,
He wants to buy my inventions and tell the world
They're his.

The decision has been made
No more negotiations to be done,
I'm now his silent partner, his hired gun,
The end will have to justify the means on this one,
It's his money and my imagination.

Made a deal with the devil, way too quick,
Under duress, to my own debit.
Amazing how far you can get in life,
As long as you are willing to do all the work
And let someone else take all the credit.

Born on third base, thinking he hit a triple,
A trial-and-error kind of guy, a bumbling fool
It's just that simple.

The decision has been made
No more negotiations to be done,
I'm now his silent partner, his hired gun,
The end will have to justify the means on this one.
It's his money and my imagination.

The decision has been made
No more negotiations to be done,
I'm now his silent partner, his hired gun.
The end will have to justify the means on this one.
It's his money and my imagination,
It's his money and my imagination.

- “Money and Imagination” is the opera’s sharp-edged confrontation song, dramatizing Tesla’s bitter first alliance with Thomas Edison as a Faustian bargain between pure genius and ruthless commercial power.

- The song presents Edison not as a heroic inventor, but as the embodiment of industrial opportunism — a man Tesla quickly recognizes as arrogant, manipulative, and willing to claim ownership over the ideas of others.

- The opening lyric, “I can’t believe I’m even talking to this guy,” establishes Tesla’s immediate disdain: he sees Edison as intellectually shallow compared with true theoretical innovators, relying more on ego and business instinct than visionary insight.

- Tesla’s contempt is rooted in history: Edison’s real-world reputation for aggressive competition and appropriation aligns directly with his notorious quote, “Everyone steals in commerce and industry. I have stolen a lot myself. But at least I know how to steal,” making the song’s accusation historically resonant.

- In dramatic terms, Edison becomes the first major antagonist in Tesla’s journey — not because he lacks intelligence, but because he represents everything Tesla is not: profit-driven, politically cunning, and willing to distort truth for advantage.

- The lyric “He’ll steal my ideas in a second and claim, ‘Hey, it’s just biz!’” captures Tesla’s dawning awareness that Edison’s interest in him is transactional: he values Tesla’s genius only insofar as it can be monetized and controlled.

- “He wants to buy my inventions and tell the world they’re his” reflects Tesla’s fear that Edison’s true aim is not partnership but possession — to absorb Tesla’s brilliance into Edison’s empire and erase the inventor behind it.

- **The central refrain, “It’s his money and my imagination,” defines the unequal bargain at the heart of their relationship: Edison controls capital, infrastructure, and influence, while Tesla provides the visionary spark that makes innovation possible.**

- **This line is also thematically crucial to the opera, because it introduces one of Tesla’s lifelong tragedies: again and again, financiers and industrialists possess the resources, while Tesla provides the ideas that change the world without reaping their rewards.**

- The phrase “I’m now his silent partner, his hired gun” reveals Tesla’s painful compromise — he knows he is subordinating his independence, yet feels compelled to accept because Edison offers the only available path to bring his inventions into reality.

- “Made a deal with the devil” gives the relationship mythic weight: Tesla understands from the beginning that this alliance is morally corrosive, but necessity forces him into it.

- The lyric suggests Tesla’s inner conflict — he is painfully aware that genius without funding remains powerless, and that invention in the modern age requires entering dangerous alliances with men he neither respects nor trusts.

- **“The end will have to justify the means”** exposes Tesla rationalizing his compromise: he convinces himself that temporary submission is acceptable if it leads to the realization of his greater scientific vision.

- The biting line "Born on third base, thinking he hit a triple" is one of the song's most devastating character judgments, portraying Edison as a man born into advantage who mistakes inherited position and commercial infrastructure for original genius.

- By calling Edison "a trial-and-error kind of guy," Tesla contrasts Edison's empirical tinkering with his own higher-order theoretical imagination — implying that Edison experiments blindly while Tesla sees complete systems in his mind before they exist.

- The song also dramatizes the beginning of Tesla's education in the brutal economics of invention: brilliant ideas alone do not rule the world — money, ownership, and narrative control do.

- Musically, "Money and Imagination" works as a biting, rhythm-driven duel of intellect and power, fueled by sarcasm, resentment, and the tension of a partnership destined to collapse.

- **In the opera's larger arc, this number marks Tesla's first major compromise with corruption — the moment he enters the industrial battlefield and learns that genius without leverage can become exploitation.**

- **The tragedy beneath the song's wit is that Tesla knows exactly what Edison is, yet must proceed anyway — not because he is deceived, but because he has no other route to bring his inventions to life.**

- "Money and Imagination" becomes the opera's anthem of creative exploitation: a brilliant inventor stepping into history through a door guarded by a man he already knows cannot be trusted.

DINNER AT DELMONICO'S

An Original Rock Opera

Written by Rodgers and Rodgers

Nikola Tesla "Light It Up"

Go out tonight, Stay in tonight,
So many decisions to be made,

Stay in tonight, Or change my life tonight,
This evening could go either way.

A bowtie made of silk, Patterned in subtle stripes,
A tailcoat of midnight blue.

Cut sharply at the waist,
An evening ascot and ebony cane,
An understated gold tie pin,
Holds everything in place.

I know the game, Act disinterested, Play hard to get,
His eyes will capture this quiet, understated, unpretentious elegance,
Men are just too easy to predict.

A nightly ritual, a scientific routine,
An air of magnificence, a quiet intensity
Not just dinner but a ballet of order, precision, control
One fork, two spoons, one knife, 2 plates
Exactly nine napkins, precisely in place.

Constellations of gas-lit crystal chandeliers,
Maitre d's, white-gloved waiters, white linens, gilded mirrors,
Will it be Lobster Newberg, Baked Alaska, or Chicken a la Keeme,
New York City at its finest, The place to be and be seen,
Champagne, string quartets, the energy electric, A Shakespearean show,
Life is not worth living unless you're dining at Delmonico's.

Jotting notes on slips of paper,
New York's most mysterious celebrity,
Performing calculations in the air with his fingers,
This unrivaled poet of electricity.

Who is this vision of theatrical grace,
Her voice, her laughter commands this place,
A brush between passion and beauty
A chance encounter or a predetermined fate.

I will accidentally pass by his table
My gloves delicately falling to the floor,
Act aloof but approachable, in the most disarming way,
He'll invite me to his table,
By the end of the night, he will ask me to stay.

A table by myself, off to the side,
Positioned by a window to observe the crowd,
Keeping my thoughts to myself, never, ever wondering out loud.

A confluence of passion and beauty
artistry and science, a spark could ignite, A magnetic force,
Playing out at Demonico's tonight.

Constellations of gas-lit crystal chandeliers.
Maitre d's, white-gloved waiters, white linens, gilded mirrors,
Will it be Lobster Newberg, Baked Alaska, or Chicken a la Keeme,
New York City at its finest, The place to be and be seen,
Champagne, string quartets, the energy electric, A Shakespearean show,
Life is not worth living unless you're dining at Delmonico's.

Constellations of gas-lit crystal chandeliers.
Maitre d's, white-gloved waiters, white linens, gilded mirrors,
Will it be Lobster Newberg, Baked Alaska, or Chicken a la Keeme,
New York City at its finest, The place to be and be seen.
Champagne, string quartets, the energy electric, A Shakespearean show,
Life is not worth living unless you're dining at Delmonico's
Life is not worth living unless you're dining at Delmonico's

• “Dinner at Delmonico’s” is the opera’s sparkling romantic-comic centerpiece — a playful, elegant change of tone that reveals Tesla not as the solemn prophet of electricity, but as an unexpectedly desirable and enigmatic man in New York society.

• The song dramatizes the famous imagined encounter between Nikola Tesla and the legendary actress Sarah Bernhardt, built around Sarah’s carefully orchestrated plan to engineer a “chance” meeting with him at Delmonico’s.

• Sarah Bernhardt is portrayed as confident, glamorous, and theatrical — a woman accustomed to commanding stages and hearts — yet Tesla presents a challenge unlike any man she has pursued before.

• Her strategy of deliberately dropping her gloves is classic theatrical seduction: a staged accident designed to force intimacy, allowing elegance and flirtation to disguise deliberate romantic pursuit.

• The lyric “Act disinterested, play hard to get” reflects Sarah’s amused awareness of courtship as performance art — she is directing this encounter like a scene in one of her own plays.

• Tesla, meanwhile, is depicted as a creature of ritual and precision: his nightly dinners at Delmonico’s are treated almost as sacred ceremony, reflecting his real-life obsession with order, symmetry, and numerical exactness.

• The lyric describing “one fork, two spoons, one knife, two plates, exactly nine napkins” beautifully captures Tesla’s compulsive precision and transforms his eccentric habits into theatrical charm.

• Delmonico’s itself becomes a glamorous character in the song — a gilded world of chandeliers, white-gloved service, mirrored opulence, and Gilded Age splendor where romance, wealth, and invention mingle under one roof.

• The references to Lobster Newberg, Baked Alaska, and especially Chicken à la Keene celebrate Delmonico’s culinary mythology: these dishes evoke the restaurant’s status as the crown jewel of New York dining and reinforce the luxurious social world Tesla inhabited.

• Chicken à la Keene is especially meaningful because it was named after James R. Keene, the wealthy financier and polo magnate associated with Delmonico’s elite clientele — underscoring that Tesla dined among America’s most powerful social and financial circles.

• The line “New York’s most mysterious celebrity” captures Tesla’s magnetic status in the city: he is both public legend and private enigma, a man famous enough to fascinate everyone yet emotionally inaccessible.

• Sarah sees Tesla not merely as a romantic prospect, but as an irresistible contradiction: a man of science who carries himself like a poet, austere yet magnetic, detached yet deeply compelling.

• Tesla’s silent habit of jotting notes and calculating in the air with his fingers turns his scientific genius into a flirtatious mystique — his mind itself becomes part of his allure.

• The song thrives on dual perspectives: Sarah is actively plotting seduction, while Tesla remains withdrawn, observant, and unaware that he is the subject of an elegant ambush.

• “A confluence of passion and beauty, artistry and science” defines the deeper thematic purpose of the scene: Sarah and Tesla represent two different forms of genius — theatrical artistry and scientific imagination — colliding in one enchanted evening.

• Dramatically, the song gives the audience relief from heavier emotional numbers by allowing wit, glamour, romance, and humor to take center stage.

- Beneath its playful charm lies poignancy: the audience understands that Tesla's emotional reserve will ultimately prevent this flirtation from becoming lasting romance, making the scene deliciously bittersweet.

- Musically, the repeated Delmonico's chorus functions like a champagne toast — lush, exuberant, and theatrical — turning the restaurant into a metaphor for a dazzling world where anything seems possible for one glittering night.

- **In the opera's larger arc, "Dinner at Delmonico's" reminds us that Tesla was not merely an inventor and martyr, but a charismatic cultural icon whose presence electrified salons, dining rooms, and hearts alike.**

- **The song becomes a joyous theatrical flirtation — a sparkling Gilded Age pas de deux in which romance almost happens, and that almost is what makes it irresistible.**

I am the Original Wizard of Oz

Written by Rodgers and Rodgers

NIKOLA TESLA

"LIGHT IT UP"

AN ORIGINAL ROCK OPERA

Welcome to the World's Fair,
The Columbian Exhibition,
I have a gift for everyone here tonight,
Straight from my imagination.

The second I throw this switch,
Two hundred thousand lights will be lit,
One for every millennial of mankind,
Who cursed the night,
Waiting for the sun to rise.

Attention all in the Court of Honor,
To Buffalo Bill's Wild West Show,
Who have ever dreamt of an emerald city,
Seth has been dealt the fatal blow.
Fountains shooting skyward,
As cannons sound,
The first American automobile,
George Ferris's new spinning wheel.

Electric sun will rise at night,
Illuminating the Champs-Elysees,
The Streets of Rome, Piccadilly's Square,
The lights on Broadway,
Beckoning Dorothy, Tin Man, Lion and Scarecrow,
To the end of the Yellow Brick Road.
The Merlin behind the curtain, the electrical god,
I am the Original Wizard of OZ.

Handel's Hallelujah Chorus will sing,
You are a witness to impossible dreams,
The most spectacular display of lights,
The world has ever seen.
Time to celebrate, but no time to rest,
You can't imagine what happens next,
The greatest inventions lay just ahead,
I just haven't thought of them yet.
What Thor and Zeus could not create,
Light it up, we must not wait.

Electric sun will rise at night,
Illuminating the Champs-Elysees,
The Streets of Rome, Piccadilly Square,
The lights on Broadway.
Beckoning Dorothy, Tin Man, Lion, and Scarecrow,
To the end of the Yellow Brick Road.
The Merlin behind the curtain, the electrical god,
I am the Original Wizard of OZ.
The Merlin behind the curtain, the electrical god,
I am the Original Wizard of OZ

• “I Am the Original Wizard of OZ” is the opera’s grand coronation anthem — Tesla at the summit of triumph, standing before the world not as a struggling outsider or embattled inventor, but as the undisputed master of modern electricity.

• This song marks Tesla’s most glorious public victory: he has defeated Thomas Edison in the War of Currents, vindicated alternating current, and transformed his dream of harnessing the power of Niagara Falls into reality.

• Niagara is crucial to the meaning of this song because it represents Tesla’s childhood vision fulfilled — as a boy he imagined taming the falls for human use, and now that dream has become a civilization-altering fact.

• **The setting is the opening night of the World’s Columbian Exposition on May 1, 1893, at the Court of Honor in Chicago — one of the most iconic public demonstrations of electrical power in history.**

• **In dramatic terms, Tesla is no longer speaking to financiers or rivals; he is addressing humanity itself, assembled before him in awe, as prophet and magician unveiling a new age.**

• “Welcome to the World’s Fair… I have a gift for everyone here tonight, straight from my imagination” frames Tesla not merely as inventor, but as benefactor to mankind — the giver of light itself.

• The act of throwing the switch that ignites 200,000 electric bulbs becomes ritualistic and almost divine: Tesla is cast as the bringer of artificial sun, turning night into radiant day before a stunned civilization.

• The lyric “One for every millennial of mankind who cursed the night waiting for the sun to rise” elevates this moment beyond technology — it becomes the symbolic end of humanity’s ancient dependence on darkness.

• Electricity here is not just utility; it is liberation from one of the oldest limits imposed on human life.

• The callout to Buffalo Bill’s Wild West Show grounds the song in the astonishing sensory overload of the fair, where spectacle, entertainment, invention, and national ambition collided on one dazzling stage.

• By naming Buffalo Bill directly, Tesla is theatrically claiming the attention of all America’s mythic frontiers — announcing that even the romance of the Wild West must now yield to the greater frontier of electricity.

• The line “Who have ever dreamt of an emerald city” is one of the opera’s most brilliant imaginative bridges, linking Tesla’s real-world illumination of the White City to the literary mythology of Oz.

• The interpretation is profoundly compelling: that The Wonderful Wizard of Oz may have drawn inspiration from the dazzling electric spectacle of the Columbian Exposition, where author L. Frank Baum was indeed present and deeply influenced by the fair.

• **Historians have long noted Baum’s likely inspiration from the glowing White City, whose brilliant illuminated architecture may have helped shape his vision of Emerald City — making this theatrical connection both imaginative and historically plausible.**

• **In the opera, Tesla becomes the hidden source behind Oz mythology**: the real wizard whose electric miracle made Baum’s fictional wonderland conceivable.

• This transforms the title phrase into something extraordinary — Tesla is not metaphorically the Wizard of Oz; he becomes the true archetype behind the legend.

• “Seth has been dealt the fatal blow” evokes the defeat of darkness itself: Seth, mythologically associated with chaos and disorder, becomes symbolic of Edison’s defeated direct current and the dying age of dim gaslight.

• **"George Ferris's new spinning wheel" is a beautiful act of inventor-to-inventor respect**, reinforcing Tesla's ethical belief that creators deserve attribution — **unlike Edison, Tesla honors the men whose ideas shape the future.**

• This detail reflects one of Tesla's defining moral differences: he always recognized genius in others and gave credit where it was due.

• "Electric sun will rise at night" is the central metaphor of the song — Tesla has achieved what once belonged only to gods: he has created a second sun under human control.

• The illumination of Paris, Rome, Piccadilly, and Broadway expands the moment globally, showing Tesla already envisioning electrification not as a local triumph, but as a worldwide transformation.

• **The invocation of Dorothy, Tin Man, Lion, and Scarecrow is theatrically ingenious because it retroactively places Tesla inside Oz mythology as its hidden progenitor — the unseen force behind Baum's enchanted world.**

• "The Merlin behind the curtain" fuses myth, technology, and theatrical illusion into one unforgettable image: Tesla is magician, engineer, and mythic wizard at once.

• Unlike Baum's fictional wizard, however, Tesla's miracles are real — his magic is science made visible.

• Calling himself "the electrical god" is not arrogance but earned dramatic apotheosis: this is the one moment in the opera where Tesla truly stands at Olympian height, having harnessed forces once reserved for Zeus and Thor.

• The lyric "Handel's Hallelujah Chorus will sing" lends sacred grandeur, making the event feel almost liturgical — the electrification of the fair becomes a kind of modern creation ceremony.

• "You are witnesses to impossible dreams" defines the emotional essence of the song: Tesla is inviting humanity to recognize that the impossible has just become reality before their eyes.

• "The greatest inventions lay just ahead, I just haven't thought of them yet" is quintessential Tesla — even at his moment of greatest triumph, his mind is already racing beyond the present into futures not yet imagined.

• This line captures his inexhaustible creativity: victory never ends invention; it only opens new doors.

• "What Thor and Zeus could not create, light it up, we must not wait," places Tesla above mythological gods in practical achievement — where ancient gods commanded lightning symbolically, Tesla has mastered it functionally for humanity's use.

• Dramatically, this song is Tesla's apotheosis scene — his transformation from inventor into legend, from scientist into cultural myth.

• Musically, this song feels monumental, triumphant, ceremonial, and ecstatic — a world-changing spectacle in sound, equal to the magnitude of the illumination itself.

• In the larger arc of the opera, this is Tesla's zenith: the moment when dream, science, public adoration, and historical destiny align perfectly before later songs reveal the cost of being so far ahead of one's time.

• **The brilliance of the Oz connection gives the song lasting theatrical magic because it reframes one of America's most beloved myths through Tesla's genius, revealing him as the hidden wizard behind modern wonder itself.**

• "I Am the Original Wizard of OZ" becomes not only Tesla's declaration of triumph, but the opera's boldest claim: that behind every great myth of magic lies the real miracle of human imagination — and Nikola Tesla was its greatest wizard.

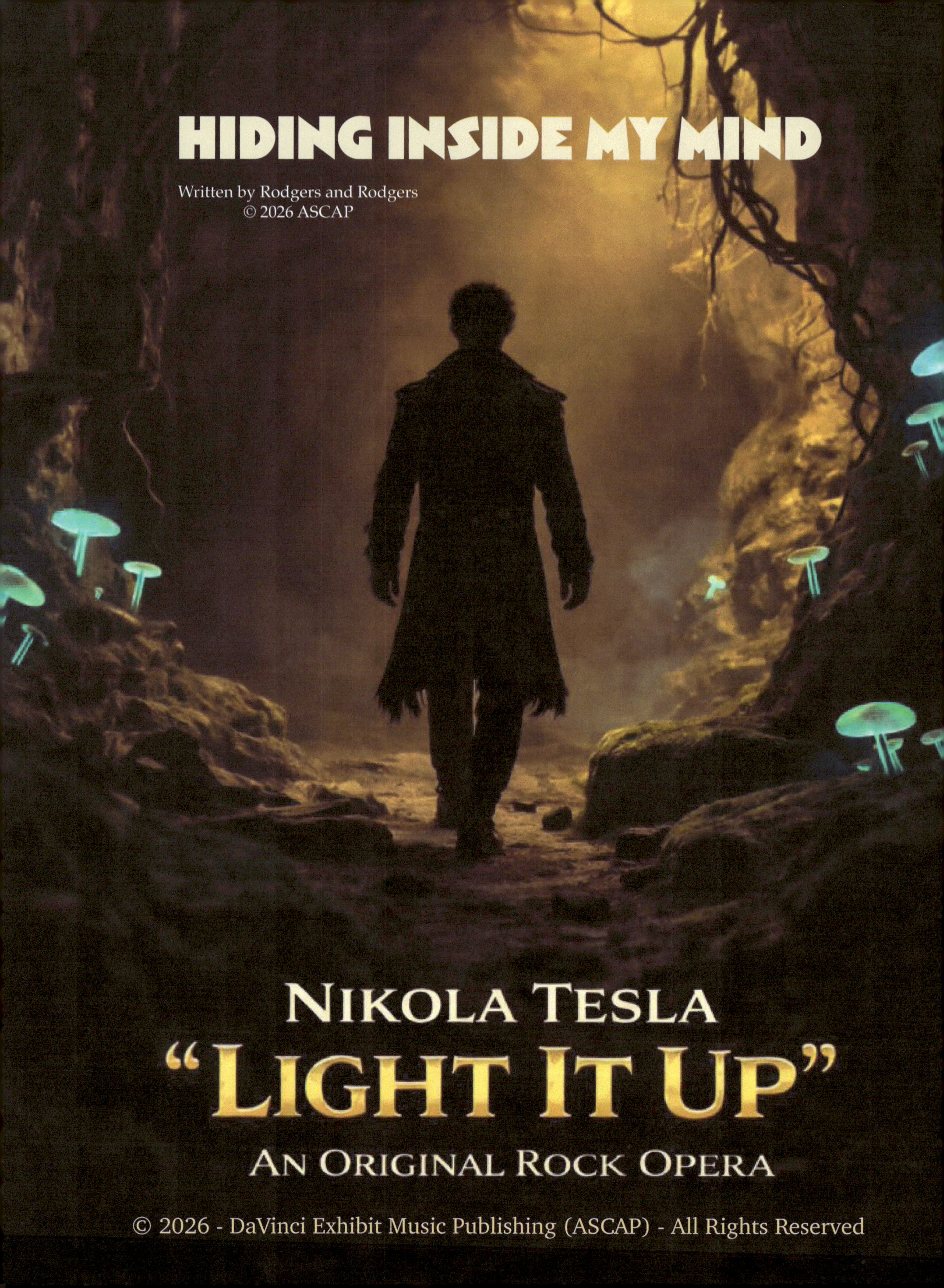
HIDING INSIDE MY MIND
Written by Rodgers and Rodgers
© 2026 ASCAP
NIKOLA TESLA
"LIGHT IT UP"
AN ORIGINAL ROCK OPERA
© 2026 - DaVinci Exhibit Music Publishing (ASCAP) - All Rights Reserved

Perceived an unperceivable spark,
That ignited this supernatural ignition,
Beguiled this novice from apprentice,
To master magician.

The inventor is himself an invention,
Receivers pointed in heaven's direction,
Unveiling gadgets, gizmos, machines, and mechanisms,
Beyond human conception.

Riding the lightning, at the top of my game,
My will and my wish are now one in the same,
Calm, cool, collected, wired to the divine,
Meandering through the labyrinth,
Hiding inside my mind.

Found the key that unlocked the lock,
I was the only one who wasn't shocked,
Just getting started, just watch.

Riding the lightning, at the top of my game,
My will and my wish are now one in the same,
Calm, cool, collected, wired to the divine
Meandering through the labyrinth,
Hiding inside my mind.

Riding the lightning, at the top of my game,
My will and my wish are now one in the same,
Calm, cool, collected, wired to the divine
Meandering through the labyrinth,
Hiding inside my mind.
Meandering through the labyrinth,
Hiding inside my mind.

• "Hiding Inside My Mind" is Tesla's triumph anthem — the moment in the opera when genius is no longer hidden in obscurity, but fully recognized in public glory after his electrifying success at the World's Columbian Exposition.

• The song celebrates Tesla at the height of his creative ascendancy: the Columbian Exhibition illumination has astonished the world, alternating current has proven its supremacy, and Tesla now stands vindicated before critics who doubted him.

• The opening image, "Perceived an unperceivable spark," reflects Tesla's extraordinary gift: his ability to see possibilities invisible to others, perceiving patterns, energies, and solutions beyond ordinary human imagination.

• "That ignited this supernatural ignition" suggests that Tesla's genius feels almost mystical — his mind operates at such an advanced level that invention appears less mechanical than transcendent.

• The phrase "from apprentice to master magician" dramatizes Tesla's transformation from struggling outsider into commanding visionary, elevating him from misunderstood immigrant inventor to near-mythic architect of the future.

• The line "The inventor is himself an invention" comes directly from Tesla's own philosophy and is central to the song's meaning: Tesla sees the inventor not merely as maker of machines, but as a being who must constantly reinvent himself to match the scale of his visions.

• This quote reveals Tesla's self-awareness — he understands that his mind itself is his greatest creation, shaped and refined as deliberately as any machine he builds.

• "Receivers pointed in heaven's direction" evokes both literal wireless experimentation and spiritual symbolism: Tesla's inventions seem to draw signals not just from nature, but from the cosmos itself.

• The cascade of "gadgets, gizmos, machines, and mechanisms beyond human conception" captures the overwhelming flood of ideas now pouring from Tesla's imagination — this is the season of abundance when his mind is producing faster than the world can absorb.

• The repeated refrain "Riding the lightning, at the top of my game" is a declaration of mastery: Tesla is no longer chasing possibility — he is commanding it. Lightning, once a metaphor for untamed force, is now his medium of expression.

• "My will and my wish are now one in the same," another authentic Tesla quote, expresses his highest state of creative achievement: the perfect union between imagination and execution, where thought and invention become instantaneous partners.

• This line is philosophically profound because it represents Tesla's ultimate artistic-scientific ideal — the ability to bring every inner vision into reality without compromise or limitation.

• "Calm, cool, collected, wired to the divine" portrays Tesla in a rare state of serenity and total confidence: he is centered, assured, and spiritually aligned with the forces he manipulates.

• The title phrase "Hiding inside my mind" reveals the true setting of the song: Tesla's greatest laboratory is not a building, but the labyrinth of his own consciousness, where inventions are fully formed before they ever touch the physical world.

• "Found the key that unlocked the lock" symbolizes breakthrough — Tesla has crossed from possibility into mastery, unlocking the mechanism that allows imagination to become world-changing reality.

- The lyric “I was the only one who wasn’t shocked” is both literal and brilliantly ironic: while the public marvels at the electrical wonder he has unleashed, Tesla himself remains unsurprised because he always knew he could achieve it.

- This line is also a sharp, sly rebuke aimed at Edison and Tesla’s skeptics — those who doubted his alternating current system are now forced to witness its triumph, while Tesla stands serenely vindicated.

- The phrase “Just getting started, just watch” gives the song exhilarating momentum: even after this public triumph, Tesla sees the Columbian Exhibition not as culmination, but merely the opening act of what is still to come.

- Dramatically, this song is essential because it places Tesla in his fullest power — intellectually, emotionally, and spiritually — before later songs reveal the costs and sacrifices attached to such genius.

- Musically, “Hiding Inside My Mind” feels expansive, soaring, and electric — a celebratory surge of confidence that lets the audience experience the thrill of standing inside Tesla’s imagination at maximum voltage.

- **In the opera’s larger arc, this is Tesla’s mountaintop moment: the world is finally seeing what he has always known, that his mind is not simply inventive — it is a universe unto itself.**

- **“Hiding Inside My Mind” becomes the ecstatic portrait of genius in full bloom: the sound of a man whose inner world is now lighting the outer one.**

- Lyrics also inspired by Caitlin Mae Rodgers

COLORADO COSMIC COWBOY

Written by Rodgers and Rodgers
© 2026 ASCAP

Nikola Tesla
"LIGHT IT UP"
An Original Rock Opera

Head west to Denver,
South to the Springs,
Up close to the power source,
Of what only nature brings.

With my rope of wire,
To lasso electric riding by,
While prospectors are panning for gold,
I'll be mining the sky.

Pikes Peak to Paris, at lightning speed,
Conducting the cosmos, playing my symphony.
Mile High in the Rockies, as far as my mind can see,
They'll conjure up a new name, just for me.
A Colorado Cosmic Cowboy, that's me.
A Colorado Cosmic Cowboy, that's me!

My gun belt of dynamos, switches, and coils,
May seem a little strange,
But it's all this Wrangler needs,
To tame the Front Range.

Thunderbolts strike far off in the distance,
By my calculations, they'll be here in an instantance.
Corral celestial gods, in their own celestial land,
Command them off and on, with the wave of my hand.

Pikes Peak to Paris, at lightning speed,
Conducting the cosmos, playing my symphony.
Mile High in the Rockies, as far as my mind can see,
They'll conjure up a new name just for me.
A Colorado Cosmic Cowboy, that's me.
A Colorado Cosmic Cowboy, that's me!

- “Colorado Cosmic Cowboy” is the opera’s mythic frontier song — a high-voltage adventure anthem that transforms Tesla’s move to Colorado Springs into the legend of a scientific outlaw riding into the American West to capture lightning itself.

- The song dramatizes Tesla’s real 1899 journey to Colorado Springs, where he built his experimental high-voltage laboratory to test wireless transmission on a scale impossible in New York, bringing him closer than ever to his dream of global energy transmission.

- In the opera, Colorado becomes Tesla’s frontier wilderness — a place where science and myth merge, and where he leaves behind civilization to confront nature on its own elemental ground.

- “Head west to Denver, south to the Springs” gives the song the cadence of a Western trail ballad, framing Tesla as a lone pioneer traveling not for land or gold, but for discovery beyond human precedent.

- The lyric “Up close to the power source of what only nature brings” captures Tesla’s purpose: to move nearer to the raw electrical forces of the earth and sky, where lightning becomes both laboratory subject and cosmic partner.

- “With my rope of wire to lasso electric riding by” brilliantly reimagines Tesla as a cowboy inventor, replacing horse and cattle with currents and bolts — he is literally attempting to rope lightning from the heavens.

- The Western metaphor deepens Tesla’s mythic identity: while prospectors mine for gold, Tesla declares, “I’ll be mining the sky,” revealing that his treasure is not mineral wealth, but energy itself.

- The refrain “Pikes Peak to Paris, at lightning speed” expresses Tesla’s extraordinary ambition — he is envisioning instantaneous wireless transmission across continents, imagining signals leaping from the Rockies to Europe decades before such systems became reality.

- This line symbolizes Tesla’s belief that distance itself could be conquered by electricity: geography would become irrelevant in a connected world powered by wireless communication.

- “Conducting the cosmos, playing my symphony” portrays Tesla as maestro rather than mechanic — not merely inventing machines, but orchestrating universal forces into harmonious technological music.

- The title “Colorado Cosmic Cowboy” captures the joy and swagger of Tesla at one of his boldest moments: he is explorer, scientist, and mythic frontiersman all at once, inventing a new kind of American hero.

- “My gun belt of dynamos, switches, and coils” replaces frontier weapons with scientific instruments, turning Tesla’s laboratory equipment into the tools of a futuristic gunslinger armed not with bullets, but electricity.

- The lyric “To tame the Front Range” suggests that Tesla’s challenge is nothing less than subduing the untamable — harnessing the raw natural violence of the Rockies and their storms into usable human power.

- The song draws directly from the famous Colorado Springs experiments in which Tesla generated enormous artificial lightning discharges, some reaching astonishing lengths, creating spectacles so immense they seemed supernatural even to witnesses.

- One legendary night, Tesla’s experiments overloaded the Colorado Springs power plant and blew out the city’s electric grid, plunging the town into darkness — a real event that underscores the dangerous scale of his ambition.

- The utility company reportedly warned Tesla not to repeat such a feat, reinforcing the idea that his experiments were already exceeding the limits of existing infrastructure.

- **The line “Thunderbolts strike far off in the distance, by my calculations they’ll be here in an instant”** reflects Tesla’s uncanny predictive relationship with electrical storms — he was no passive observer, but an active interpreter of nature’s timing and patterns.

- **“Corral celestial gods in their own celestial land”** elevates Tesla into mythic territory: he is no longer simply studying lightning, but commanding the gods themselves, as though Zeus has handed him the reins.

- The most profound historical revelation behind this song is Tesla’s discovery that electrical currents could travel through the earth itself — a breakthrough he believed proved his dream of global wireless energy was physically possible.

- During one dangerous experiment, Tesla and his assistant came close to death amid overwhelming electrical discharge, underscoring the perilous intensity of his work and his willingness to risk everything for discovery.

- At the climax of these experiments, Tesla placed large incandescent bulbs directly into the ground, and they illuminated without wires — a moment of revelation proving to him that the earth itself could function as a conductor.

- Nearby horses reportedly received mild shocks through their hooves, a vivid sign that Tesla had succeeded in energizing the ground itself and was witnessing the planet become part of his electrical circuit.

- **This moment is pivotal in Tesla’s life and in the opera’s dramatic arc**: it is here that his dream of transmitting free wireless power to the entire globe becomes not fantasy, but scientific conviction.

- Musically, the song feels exuberant, swaggering, and cinematic — blending Western imagery with cosmic grandeur to create one of the opera’s most visually exhilarating numbers.

- In the larger structure of the opera, “Colorado Cosmic Cowboy” is Tesla’s conquest song: the moment he becomes not merely inventor of machines, but master of elemental force, proving to himself that the earth can indeed be electrified.

- **The emotional power of the song lies in its fearless optimism — here Tesla is still riding toward possibility, convinced that the universe itself is ready to yield its secrets to him.**

- “Colorado Cosmic Cowboy” becomes the electrified frontier myth of the opera: Tesla as lone rider beneath storm-filled skies, chasing lightning toward the future and finding that the whole earth is waiting to light up beneath his feet.

WARDENCLYFFE

Written by Rodgers and Rodgers

NIKOLA TESLA
"LIGHT IT UP"
AN ORIGINAL ROCK OPERA

A three-hour train ride from Midtown to Shoreham,
On cliffs, overlooking Long Island Sound,
Then an hour-long carriage ride through the countryside,
Transforming Wardenclyffe's farmers' field,
Where the next wonder of the world will be found.

A wireless system for communication and power,
A grand vision, a one hundred eighty-seven-foot wooden tower.
A fifty-five-ton steel sphere on top,
Covered with a thin layer of copper, A shaft with sixteen iron pipes.
Driven one hundred feet into the ground,
Currents, vibrations will seize hold of the earth,
An endless river, Wardenclyffe will deliver
The planet itself will begin to quiver.

No mortal or deity ever imagined or asked, Oooooh
Never undertook such a Herculean task, Oooooh
A worldwide, free distribution of energy,
Connecting all the corners of the globe, Wherever you may be.

No mortal or deity ever imagined or asked, Oooooh
Never undertook such a Herculean task, Oooooh
A worldwide, free distribution of energy,
Connecting all the corners of the globe, Wherever you may be.
Oooooh. Ooooooh, Ohoooo Wherever you may be,
Oooooh. Ooooooh, Ohoooo Wherever you may be
The powers that be, Don't want humanity free,
They want all the gold, they never quit What don't these guys get?
They are tearing down Wardenclyffe.

Three, six, nine, Living life by the numbers,To achieve a great result is one thing,
To achieve it at the right time, Is another.

Television transmissions, movies, images, sent simultaneously,
Telephone calls, pictures, seeing and hearing one another instantaneously,
Warnings, signals, messages, SOS's, will be flying through the ether,
And all JP Morgan could ask was, "Where is the meter?"

No mortal or deity ever imagined or asked, Oooooh
Never undertook such a Herculean task, Oooooh
A worldwide, free distribution of energy,
Connecting all the corners of the globe, Wherever you may be.

No mortal or deity ever imagined or asked, Oooooh
Never undertook such a Herculean task, Oooooh
A worldwide, free distribution of energy,
Connecting all the corners of the globe, Wherever you may be.
Oooooooh, The powers that be, Oooooh, The powers that be,
Oooooh, Don't want humanity free,
They want all the gold, they never quit,
What don't these guys get? They are tearing down Wardenclyffe.

No mortal or deity ever imagined or asked, Ooooooh
Never undertook such a Herculean task, Ooooooh
A worldwide, free distribution of energy,
Connecting all the corners of the globe, Wherever you may be.
Oooooh. Ooooooh, Ohoooo Wherever you will,
Ooooooh, aaaaah, Ooooooh Wherever you will,
Ooooooh, aaaaah, Ooooooh Wherever you will,
Ooooooh, aaaaah, Ooooooh Wherever you will,

The powers that be, Don't want humanity free,
They want all the gold, they never quit What don't these guys get?
They are tearing down Wardenclyffe.

Oooooh. Ooooooh, Ohoooo Wherever you will,
Ooooooh, aaaaah, Ooooooh Wherever you will,
Ooooooh, aaaaah, Ooooooh Wherever you will,
Ooooooh, aaaaah, Ooooooh Wherever you will.

- “Wardenclyffe” is the opera’s grand monument to Tesla’s most visionary dream: not merely a machine or invention, but his attempt to reshape civilization itself through universal wireless communication and free global energy.

- The song opens cinematically with the journey from Manhattan to Shoreham, tracing Tesla’s pilgrimage from the center of commerce to the edge of possibility — from crowded modernity into open land where imagination can become reality.

- The remote Long Island site becomes sacred dramatic ground: a humble farmer’s field transformed into the birthplace of what Tesla believed would become one of humanity’s greatest technological wonders.

- The detailed physical description of the tower — its 187-foot wooden frame, 55-ton steel sphere clad in copper, and sixteen iron shafts driven deep into the earth — emphasizes that Wardenclyffe was not fantasy, but a real and monumental engineering undertaking grounded in scientific precision.

- The recurring chorus line, **“No mortal or deity ever imagined or asked,”** expresses the radical scale of Tesla’s vision: he was conceiving something so unprecedented that neither ordinary humanity nor even mythic gods had imagined such a possibility.

- This lyric defines Tesla’s isolation as a visionary — his ideas are so far beyond contemporary thought that language itself struggles to contain them; he is operating beyond the horizon of collective imagination.

- “Never undertook such a Herculean task” frames Tesla as a mythic figure, comparable to Hercules, attempting a labor beyond human precedent: not conquering beasts, but conquering the invisible forces of the earth itself.

- In dramatic terms, the chorus elevates Wardenclyffe from engineering project to cosmic undertaking — Tesla is not simply building a tower; he is trying to wire the planet into one unified living system.

- The promise of “a worldwide, free distribution of energy, connecting all the corners of the globe” captures Tesla’s deepest humanitarian ideal: a world in which energy and communication flow freely to all people, unrestricted by wealth, borders, or monopoly.

- The song reveals how astonishingly prophetic Tesla’s vision was: television transmission, wireless telephone calls, images sent instantly, global messaging, and live audiovisual communication all anticipate the modern internet, video calls, mobile networks, and satellite communication decades before their realization.

- The line “Warnings, signals, messages, SOS’s will be flying through the ether” demonstrates Tesla’s uncanny foresight into a connected digital civilization — a world we now inhabit, though few in his own era could comprehend it.

- **J.P. Morgan’s devastating question, “Where is the meter?”** becomes the central conflict of the song: Tesla imagines universal human benefit, while financiers demand monetization, exposing the irreconcilable clash between visionary idealism and profit-driven capitalism.

- “The powers that be don’t want humanity free” expresses Tesla’s growing realization that his greatest obstacle is not science, but entrenched economic systems that fear any invention that cannot be controlled, rationed, or sold.

- The repeated lament “They are tearing down Wardenclyffe” is both literal and symbolic: it refers to the tower’s destruction, but also to the dismantling of Tesla’s dream for a freer and more equitable world.

- The numerical line “Three, six, nine, living life by the numbers” invokes Tesla’s mystical fascination with mathematical harmony, suggesting that Wardenclyffe was not only technological but spiritual — an attempt to align human civilization with universal natural law.

- Musically, the recurring soaring chorus gives the number cathedral-like grandeur, making the audience feel the awe of standing inside a dream too large for its own century.

- In the opera's dramatic arc, "Wardenclyffe" is Tesla at his most Promethean: reaching beyond invention into world transformation, daring to give humanity what history was not yet prepared to receive.

- The tragedy of the song lies in its paradox: Tesla succeeds in imagining the future with astonishing clarity, yet fails to persuade his own time to believe in it.

- "Wardenclyffe" becomes the opera's ultimate anthem of unrealized possibility — a towering elegy for the greatest future that almost was.

- **Control of Patents:** In exchange for his initial investment, Morgan received a **51% stake** in Tesla's wireless patents

- This effectively "locked" Tesla's intellectual property, making it difficult for him to find other major investors without Morgan's approval.

- **Communication vs. Power:** Morgan specifically wanted a high-speed communications network for business and maritime use . He felt misled when he discovered Tesla was actually building a "World Power System" that would disrupt established energy monopolies—including those Morgan himself had interests in

- **Breakdown of Relationship:** As funding dried up, Tesla wrote increasingly desperate letters to Morgan, pleading for support and claiming his work would "advance the world a century"

- Morgan eventually refused to communicate directly, replying only through his secretary that further assistance was "impossible."

- The tower was eventually dynamited in 1917 to pay off Tesla's mounting debts at the Waldorf-Astoria Hotel.

'LIARS, THIEVES, KNAVES, HIGH-WAYMEN, AND BANDITOS'

Written by Rodgers and Rodgers

NIKOLA TESLA

"LIGHT IT UP"

AN ORIGINAL ROCK OPERA

The future will tell the truth,
Judge each man by his work and merit,
The present is theirs, the future is mine,
Mastering nature's forces, without taking credit.

An unexpected turn of events,
A twist of fate for fortune's fool,
Billion-dollar corporations created,
And I can't even pay my bills.

Turbines, transmitters, neon lights,
Robots, radios, and radar controls,
Gave away everything to everyone, even my soul,
Whatever was left over, they stole.
they're all,
Liars, thieves, knaves, highwaymen, and banditos.

Only have myself to blame, forced to vacate
The Waldorf Astoria and St. Regis,
No one now to look after my own best self-interests,

If only John Jacob Astor hadn't gone down with the
Titanic,
Rewards are in proportion with work and sacrifice.
I'm saddened by my fellow man, to be quite frank,
Maybe someone, at some time, would simply walk up
to me
and say "Thanks,"

Turbines, transmitters, neon lights,
Robots, radios, and radar controls
Gave away everything to everyone, even my soul.
Whatever was left over, they stole. They're all
Liars, thieves, knaves, highwaymen, and banditos,
They're all liars, thieves, knaves, highwaymen, and
banditos.

- “Liars, Thieves, Knaves, Highwaymen and Banditos” captures Tesla at one of the darkest emotional turning points in the opera: a brilliant visionary now embittered by betrayal, financial ruin, and the theft of his legacy.

- **The opening lines quote Tesla directly: “The future will tell the truth…** The present is theirs, the future is mine,” establishing the song as both personal testimony and philosophical reckoning — Tesla’s defiant belief that history, not his contemporaries, will vindicate him.

- By this stage in his life, Tesla sees the modern world built upon inventions he pioneered — alternating current systems, turbines, wireless transmission, neon illumination, robotics, radio concepts, and radar principles — yet the wealth and recognition generated by these breakthroughs have gone to others.

- The refrain naming “liars, thieves, knaves, highwaymen, and banditos” is not merely anger for dramatic effect; it reflects Tesla’s real bitterness toward financiers, industrialists, and rivals who profited from his genius while excluding him from its rewards.

- The lyric “Billion-dollar corporations created, and I can’t even pay my bills” underscores the tragic paradox of Tesla’s life: the architect of modern electrical civilization dies nearly penniless while empires are built on his ideas.

- “Gave away everything to everyone, even my soul” reflects Tesla’s pattern of sacrificing personal profit for the sake of advancing humanity — he repeatedly relinquished patents, rights, and financial leverage because he believed invention should serve mankind, not greed.

- The reference to being forced to vacate the Waldorf Astoria New York and the St. Regis New York recalls Tesla’s real decline into financial instability, when unpaid debts led to eviction from the grand hotels where he once lived as a celebrated celebrity inventor.

- John Jacob Astor IV, Tesla’s patron and admirer, is central to the song’s grief: Astor believed in Tesla’s genius and provided vital financial backing, but his death in the RMS Titanic sinking cut off one of Tesla’s last great champions.

- The line “If only John Jacob Astor hadn’t gone down with the Titanic” is both literal and symbolic — Astor’s death represents the collapse of Tesla’s remaining bridge to financial security and institutional support.

- Tesla’s lament is not driven only by money, but by wounded dignity: beneath the anger lies heartbreak that the world embraced his inventions while forgetting the man behind them.

- **The line “Maybe someone, at some time, would simply walk up to me and say ‘Thanks’”** is the emotional core of the song — a devastatingly human plea for acknowledgment after a lifetime spent giving civilization its future.

- Dramatically, this song reveals Tesla stripped of idealistic innocence: no longer the radiant prophet of progress, he is now confronting the cruel economics of innovation and the loneliness of being ahead of one’s time.

- Musically, the pounding repetition of the chorus functions like an accusation hurled at history itself — Tesla becomes prosecutor, witness, and victim in the trial of a world that exploited him.

- In the opera's larger arc, **this number is essential because it exposes the personal cost of genius**: invention may change the world, but the inventor may be left broken by the very society he transformed.
- "Liars, Thieves, Knaves, Highwaymen and Banditos" becomes Tesla's bitter anthem of reckoning — a thunderous cry from a man whose greatest tragedy is not failure, but being indispensable and forgotten at the same time.

Written by Rodgers and Rodgers

PRESENCE

Nikola Tesla
"LIGHT IT UP"

An Original Rock Opera

A cry, recognized, traveling across the sky,
Calling me to you,
Tonight, as every night,
To see if you are alright,
Ooooooh-oo,
That is what doves do.

How were you able to find me?
How could you know where I am?
Room thirty-three twenty-seven at the New Yorker
High above the roar of Manhattan.

A genius should be fearless,
Yet, I am frightened to the bone,
You spent your life in electric dreams
The secret of invention is,
be.....alone.

Wherever we are together,
Is where we reside,
Home is not a place,
It's a presence we find.
When the last words are spoken,
When the story is written,
The greatest gift ever envisioned,
Is the power to return the love,
The love that we've been given.

So much still to achieve,
So much remains to be done,
We will never, ever let ourselves down.
We've been practicing our whole life,
We can do this in our sleep,
Oooooh,
Our ultimate encore.
We've done this all a thousand times before.
Tonight, we'll just be,
Tomorrow we will execute our strategy flawlessly.

Wherever we are together,
Is where we reside,
Home is not a place,
It's a presence we find.
When the last words are spoken,
When the story is written,
The greatest gift ever envisioned,
Is the power to return the love,
The love that we've been given.

Wherever we are together,
Is where we reside,
Home is not a place,
It's a presence we find.
When the last words are spoken,
When the story is written,
The greatest gift ever envisioned,
Is the power to return the love,
The love that we've been given.

The greatest gift ever envisioned,
Is the power to return the love,
The love that we've been given.

• In his later years at the New Yorker Hotel, Nikola Tesla formed an intense emotional bond with a white dove that regularly visited him in Room 3327, becoming one of the most poignant symbols of his solitude and inner life.

• Tesla fed and cared for pigeons daily in New York, but he spoke of one white dove in particular as unique — a being with whom he believed he shared a profound, almost mystical understanding beyond ordinary human language.

• He famously said that he "loved that pigeon as a man loves a woman," describing their connection as one of complete spiritual communion, suggesting that to him she represented companionship deeper than any earthly relationship he had known.

• Many interpreters believe Tesla may have projected into this dove the memory or spiritual essence of Katherine Johnson, the wife of his close friend Robert Underwood Johnson, for whom Tesla is widely believed to have held a deep, unspoken, platonic love.

• Katherine and Robert Johnson were among Tesla's dearest companions in New York society; they admired him not merely as an inventor, but as a rare and noble genius, offering him emotional warmth and loyalty throughout his life.

• Because Tesla never married and denied himself romantic attachment in pursuit of scientific purity, the white dove can be understood in the opera as the embodiment of love transformed into spirit — a vessel for affection he could never openly claim in human form.

• In "Presence," the dove becomes more than a bird: she is memory, longing, transcendence, and grace — arriving in his room as a silent messenger between the earthly and the eternal.

• Tesla said that when the dove came to him in her final visit, light shone from her eyes "more intense than any lamp," and in that moment he knew that something central in his life had ended.

• In the dramatic arc of the opera, the white dove symbolizes Tesla's final intimate connection to love itself — a luminous presence that comforts him as the world fades and his earthly journey nears its close.

• In his final years at the New Yorker Hotel, Tesla's white dove becomes not merely a cherished bird, but his last true confidante — a spiritual companion who seeks him out in Room 3327 high above Manhattan, answering his loneliness with unwavering devotion.

• In "Presence," **the relationship is dramatized as an intimate dialogue between Tesla and the dove**, each comforting the other in a moment of mutual tenderness, as though they are two souls who have always belonged together beyond ordinary time.

• The dove's nightly journey across the sky symbolizes loyalty, transcendence, and unconditional love — she comes not out of instinct, but out of conscious care, "to see if you are alright," making her both guardian and witness to Tesla's final days.

• Tesla's question — "How were you able to find me?" — reveals wonder not only at her physical arrival, but at the mystery of spiritual connection: she finds him because their bond transcends place, distance, and earthly boundaries.

• The song reveals one of Tesla's deepest personal truths: "The secret of invention is... be alone." This becomes a central philosophical confession in the opera — Tesla acknowledges that the solitude required for genius has also been the source of his pain and isolation.

- In this moment, the dove understands what the world never fully grasped: that Tesla's brilliance was born in silence, in separation from ordinary human attachment, and that genius often comes at the cost of companionship.

- **The lyric "Wherever we are together, is where we reside — home is not a place, it's a presence we find" transforms the dove into the embodiment of emotional home, suggesting that Tesla's true refuge is not geography, but communion with the one being who truly knows him.**

- The dove may also be interpreted as the spiritual echo of Katherine Johnson — the unattainable, platonic love Tesla carried quietly in his heart — making the bird a poetic vessel for love that could never fully take human form.

- The repeated theme of "returning the love we've been given" gives the song its emotional center: Tesla, who gave light to the world, is finally receiving light back in the form of devotion, tenderness, and presence.

- The line **"We've done this all a thousand times before"** gives the scene a timeless, almost reincarnational quality, suggesting that their bond exists beyond one lifetime — eternal, practiced, and unbroken.

- In the dramatic arc of the opera, **"Presence" becomes Tesla's most vulnerable revelation**: beneath the inventor, the visionary, and the myth is a man whose greatest need was not recognition, but love returned.

- The song turns the white dove into the final keeper of Tesla's soul — the luminous presence that remains with him when all else has fallen away.

STANDING ON MY GRAVE

Written by Rodgers and Rodgers

Nikola Tesla

"LIGHT IT UP"

An Original Rock Opera

I imagine a day like any other,
The sunrise, a muted red.
The only difference from yesterday is
I'll be dead.

Pallbearers, priests, hurst and processions,
Coffin and candles, no more earthly possessions.
What all this means, can't figure this funeral thing out,
You'd think we'd have it down a little better by now.

Praised and criticized by friend and foe,
Even from people I've never known,
I don't care that they stole my ideas,
I care they had none of their own.

Wizard or warlock, knight, or knave,
Wonder what they'll say,
Standing on my grave.
Wizard or warlock, knight, or knave,
Wonder what they'll say,
Standing on my grave.

I'll be reincarnated as a stranger,
An old friend of the deceased.
To pay my final respects, to myself,
In hopes, I can somehow now rest in peace.

The last rights are about to begin,
Wonder is there an afterlife or is this really the end.
No immediate family, no next of kin,
My inventions, my offspring, are my children.

Wizard or warlock, knight, or knave,
Wonder what they'll say
Standing on my grave.

- “Standing On My Grave” is Tesla’s elegiac meditation on mortality — one of the opera’s most intimate and philosophical songs, in which the great inventor sits alone in Room 3327 of the New Yorker Hotel, imagining the day the world must finally say goodbye to him.

- Unlike earlier songs driven by conquest, invention, or confrontation, this number is stripped of spectacle; here, Tesla is no longer battling rivals or harnessing lightning — he is confronting the one force no genius can overcome: death itself.

- The opening line, “I imagine a day like any other, the sunrise, a muted red,” is haunting in its simplicity: Tesla envisions death not as a dramatic catastrophe, but as a quiet absence — the ordinary world continuing without him.

- “The only difference from yesterday is I’ll be dead” captures the stark humility of the lyric: for a man who transformed civilization, death still arrives with unsettling plainness, indifferent to greatness.

- This perspective reveals Tesla’s detached intellectual nature — even in contemplating his own death, he observes it almost scientifically, as though studying the event from outside himself.

- The funeral imagery — pallbearers, priests, hearses, processions, candles — is presented not with reverence, but with puzzled skepticism, reflecting Tesla’s lifelong tendency to question rituals others accept without thought.

- The line “What all this means, can’t figure this funeral thing out, you’d think we’d have it down a little better by now” is profoundly Tesla-like: even death ceremonies are subjected to his analytical scrutiny, as if human custom itself is an unsolved design flaw.

- This lyric reveals both irony and vulnerability — Tesla, master of systems and forces, cannot find rational coherence in the rituals surrounding mortality.

- “Praised and criticized by friend and foe, even from people I’ve never known” captures the contradictory public life Tesla endured: adored, misunderstood, mythologized, dismissed, and debated by admirers and detractors alike.

- The line reflects his awareness that legacy is never owned by the dead — once gone, reputation belongs to those who interpret, distort, praise, or condemn from afar.

- The direct quote “I don’t care that they stole my ideas, I care they had none of their own” is one of Tesla’s sharpest and most enduring statements, and in this song it functions as his final moral judgment on those who profited from imitation without true vision.

- This line is not merely bitterness — it is Tesla’s ultimate assertion that originality is the true measure of genius, and theft of ideas is less tragic than the absence of imagination itself.

- In the context of the song, it becomes his last intellectual victory: even in death, he remains morally superior to those who exploited him, because his ideas came from creation, not appropriation.

- The recurring line “Wizard or warlock, knight or knave” reflects Tesla’s awareness that history has always struggled to classify him — was he a saintly genius, eccentric mystic, misunderstood prophet, dangerous radical, or brilliant outsider?

- These archetypes show how myth and reality have fused around Tesla’s image: even he wonders how posterity will choose to define him.

- “Wonder what they’ll say standing on my grave” is the emotional center of the song — Tesla is imagining the verdict history will deliver when he is no longer present to defend himself.

- This question is deeply human: after a lifetime of being doubted, misrepresented, and overshadowed, Tesla still longs to know whether truth will prevail once he is gone.

- The extraordinary lyric "I'll be reincarnated as a stranger, an old friend of the deceased, to pay my final respects to myself" reveals Tesla's uniquely metaphysical imagination.
- This image suggests a soul unable to detach from its own unfinished story — Tesla imagines returning anonymously to witness his own funeral, as though even death cannot sever his curiosity about how the world receives him.
- It is both whimsical and heartbreaking: a man so isolated in life imagines becoming his own mourner in death.
- "In hopes I can somehow now rest in peace" implies that peace has eluded Tesla throughout life — perhaps only in death might he find the stillness denied him in his restless years of invention and struggle.
- "Wonder is there an afterlife or is this really the end?" reveals Tesla's quiet spiritual uncertainty — despite his cosmic imagination, he remains honest before the mystery of death, unable to claim certainty where none exists.
- The lyric "No immediate family, no next of kin" underscores the loneliness of Tesla's final years: he leaves behind no spouse, no children, no domestic lineage in the traditional sense.
- Yet this loneliness is immediately transformed by one of the song's most beautiful lines: "My inventions, my offspring, are my children."
- Here, Tesla redefines legacy — where others leave bloodlines, he leaves civilization transformed by creations that will outlive him across centuries.
- This line gives profound dignity to his solitude: though alone in human terms, he is spiritually father to a technological world shaped by his genius.
- Dramatically, the song functions as Tesla's reckoning with immortality — not immortality of the soul, but immortality through contribution, invention, and memory.
- Musically, "Standing On My Grave" feels spacious, reflective, and haunting, allowing silence and restraint to carry as much weight as melody — it is the sound of a giant mind sitting quietly with eternity.
- In the opera's larger arc, this song is Tesla's final interior confession: no applause, no laboratories, no rivals — only a man measuring the meaning of his life against the inevitability of death.
- The tragedy and beauty of the song lie in its paradox: Tesla cannot understand the rituals of burial, yet understands perfectly what truly survives — not the body beneath stone, but the invisible current of ideas still moving through the world.
- "Standing On My Grave" becomes the opera's final philosophical mirror: a meditation on how genius is remembered, how history judges, and whether the world ever truly understands the people who change it forever.

PEACE

Written by Rodgers and Rodgers
© 2026 ASCAP

Nikola Tesla

"LIGHT IT UP"

An Original Rock Opera

Ladies and Gentlemen, I welcome you to this moment,
The consequence of my birth,
To reveal my invention of inventions,
The reason I was placed here on earth.

Imagine a particle beam so powerful,
An instrument capable of projecting a focused stream of energy across the sky,
Unimaginable until today,
Not a weapon of aggression, but protection,
An invisible shield, a Teleforce Ray.

A wall of power, a single beam,
A spear of light,
A sentinel soldier standing guard
Through the endless night.
The thunder of guns will be silenced
The tears of our mothers will cease,
We will emerge from the bonds, the shackles,
The chains of war,
War will become obsolete,
I love you all so much, PEACE!

May Jupiter Optimus Maximus
Banish Ares to Tartarus' eternal abyss,
May Mars guide humanity into an age of enlightenment,
Away from this precipice.

We've been deceived into thinking that war is somehow normal,
From the very beginning, we have been misled.
No longer will the souls of our sons and daughters,
Paint the battlefields red.

A wall of power, a single beam,
A spear of light,
A sentinel soldier standing guard
Through the endless night.
The thunder of guns will be silenced,
The tears of our mothers will cease,
We will emerge from the bonds, the shackles,
The chains of war,
War will become obsolete,
I love you all so much, PEACE!

A wall of power, a single beam,
A spear of light,
A sentinel soldier standing guard
Through the endless night.
The thunder of guns will be silenced,
The tears of our mothers will cease,
We will emerge from the bonds, the shackles,
The chains of war,
War will become obsolete,
I love you all so much, PEACE!

I love you all so much, PEACE!

- “Peace” is Tesla’s final benediction to humanity — the opera’s moral summit, where the aging inventor offers not revenge, profit, or personal vindication, but his last and greatest dream: the abolition of war itself.

- By this point in the opera, Tesla has lost wealth, status, and recognition, yet the song reveals that he has lost none of his original purpose: to use genius in the service of humanity rather than self-enrichment.

- This number returns directly to the ethical foundation planted in “Born Tesla”: the lessons of Georgina “Đuka” Tesla — kindness, service, and responsibility to mankind — now come full circle in Tesla’s final visionary act.

- The opening line, “Ladies and Gentlemen, I welcome you to this moment,” gives the song the tone of a solemn public revelation, as if Tesla is stepping once more before the world to unveil the ultimate expression of his life’s mission.

- “The consequence of my birth” is profoundly significant: Tesla frames this invention not as another project, but as the very reason he believes he was placed on earth.

- This suggests destiny fulfilled — every triumph, betrayal, and sacrifice in his life has led to this culminating gift.

- The phrase “invention of inventions” elevates Teleforce above all his previous achievements, implying that, unlike systems of light or power, this creation addresses the deepest wound in human civilization: war itself.

- Historically, Tesla’s Teleforce concept was his proposed charged-particle beam defense system, often misunderstood as a “death ray,” though Tesla himself envisioned it primarily as a deterrent weapon designed to make invasion impossible.

- In the opera, Teleforce is transformed into something spiritually larger: not merely military technology, but an instrument of planetary peace — a shield rather than a sword.

- “Not a weapon of aggression, but protection” is the moral heart of Tesla’s vision: unlike the machinery of war built for conquest, Teleforce exists to render violence futile by making nations impregnable to attack.

- The image of “an invisible shield” reframes technological power as guardianship — Tesla’s final ambition is not domination, but the preservation of life.

- The recurring metaphor “A wall of power, a single beam, a spear of light” gives the invention mythic grandeur: it is both scientific device and luminous symbol of civilization defending itself without bloodshed.

- “A sentinel soldier standing guard through the endless night” turns Teleforce into a tireless guardian, replacing armies of men with impersonal protection that never tires, fears, or kills from hatred.

- **The line “The thunder of guns will be silenced” is one of the song’s most emotionally powerful promises** — Tesla imagines a world where warfare ends not by treaty alone, but because its mechanisms become obsolete.

- “The tears of our mothers will cease” connects this song directly back to Đuka Tesla and the maternal voice of “Born Tesla,” **completing a powerful emotional circle**: the mother who gave life becomes the symbol of all mothers spared the grief of losing children to war.

- This line universalizes Tesla’s compassion — his concern is not for nations, but for human suffering at its most intimate and devastating level.

- “We will emerge from the bonds, the shackles, the chains of war” portrays war not as an inevitable human condition, but as a prison humanity has wrongly accepted as normal.

- Tesla’s vision here is revolutionary: peace is not passive absence of conflict, but liberation from an ancient system of organized violence.

- The declaration “War will become obsolete” is one of the boldest philosophical statements in the opera — Tesla is not proposing reform of war, but its extinction through technological transcendence.

- This reflects Tesla’s lifelong belief that scientific advancement should solve humanity’s greatest collective problems, not merely improve convenience or commerce.

• "I love you all so much, PEACE!" is astonishingly vulnerable and deeply moving because it strips away all scientific abstraction and reveals Tesla's naked emotional truth: beneath the inventor stands a man motivated by profound love for humanity.

• **The bridge invoking Jupiter Optimus Maximus, Ares, Mars, and Tartarus transforms the song into mythic cosmic judgment.**

• **Jupiter Optimus Maximus — supreme Roman god of justice and divine authority — is called upon as the ultimate arbiter to cast judgment upon the forces of war.**

• **Ares, representing bloodlust, aggression, and destructive warfare, becomes the embodiment of war profiteers, militarists, and those who perpetuate violence for gain.**

• **By asking Jupiter to banish Ares to Tartarus, Tesla is symbolically demanding that the spirit of war itself be condemned to the deepest abyss — not merely defeated, but exiled beyond redemption.**

• **Tartarus, in classical mythology, is the most severe realm of divine punishment, reserved for forces too dangerous to remain among gods or men, making this invocation dramatically absolute.**

• **The choice of Mars instead of Ares is profoundly meaningful:** though both are war gods, Mars in Roman tradition is also protector, guardian of civilization, and associated with disciplined defense rather than chaos and slaughter.

• **In this contrast, the lyrics create a brilliant moral distinction**: destructive war must be banished, but protective strength must remain to guide humanity responsibly.

• **"May Mars guide humanity into an age of enlightenment" redefines strength itself** — not conquest, but stewardship; not domination, but protection in service of peace.

• The line "We've been deceived into thinking war is somehow normal" is Tesla's indictment of history itself: he rejects the assumption that endless war is human destiny and challenges civilization's moral complacency.

• "From the very beginning, we have been misled" suggests that violence is not natural law but an inherited illusion — a false inevitability perpetuated by those who benefit from conflict.

• "No longer will the souls of our sons and daughters paint the battlefields red" is among the opera's most heartbreaking lines, transforming battlefield death into sacred human loss and making war's cost impossible to ignore abstractly.

• Dramatically, "Peace" is Tesla's final act of redemption: though denied wealth and recognition, he proves that his greatness lies not in what he gained, but in what he still chooses to give.

• Musically, this song feels both solemn and transcendent — part public address, part prayer, part prophetic anthem — carrying the emotional weight of a final testament offered to mankind.

• In the opera's larger arc, "Peace" is Tesla's spiritual climax: not the triumph of fame, but the triumph of purpose fulfilled.

• **The tragedy beneath the song is that Teleforce was never realized as Tesla imagined, yet the beauty of the number lies in the fact that his vision remains morally alive even if technologically incomplete.**

• **"Peace" becomes the opera's ultimate moral statement: Tesla's greatest invention is not electricity, communication, or machinery — it is the dream that genius, guided by compassion, might one day free humanity from war forever.**

'LIGHT IT UP'

Main Theme

An Original Rock Opera

Written by Rodgers and Rodgers

I'd wave my hands in front of my eyes,
To see what was real or if my mind was adrift.
What I thought was an affliction,
Turned out to be a gift.

Sensing the power of visualization,
Illuminating flashes were no hallucinations.
Only a receiver to the great unknown,
A celestial connection on a cosmic phone,
Cosmic phone.

Dream, imagine, create, and wonder,
Are all in the public domain,
An unlimited repertoire
Plays in my brain.
Harnessing the Sun can't be that tough,
I just hadn't thought hard enough.
I can feel the presence of the powers that be,
Mount Olympus is contacting me,

Cosmic Communications
Energy, frequency, and vibrations,
Power, pulsating from pole to pole,
Unleashing the world's electrical soul,
Exclaim to Erebus .... enoughs, enough,
From now to forever, Let's Light It Up!
Let's Light It Up!

You can't do that, because it can't be done
The fools would say,
Those who came to scoff would remain to pray.

Cosmic Communications
Energy, frequency, and vibrations,
Power, pulsating from pole to pole,
Unleashing the world's electrical soul,
Exclaim to Erebus .... enoughs, enough,
From now to forever ..... Let's Light It Up!
Let's Light It Up!

- "Light It Up" is the defining anthem of the entire rock opera — Tesla's credo, declaration of purpose, and ultimate manifesto of enlightenment. It is not merely the title song; it is the philosophical core of the work, where Tesla reveals the source of his genius and proclaims his mission to banish darkness from the world.

- **This song functions as Tesla's self-revelation**: it tells us not what he built, but how he experienced reality itself — how the inner workings of his mind became the birthplace of his inventions.

- The opening lyric, "I'd wave my hands in front of my eyes, to see what was real or if my mind was adrift," comes from Tesla's real childhood accounts of overwhelming visual phenomena, when brilliant flashes and mental images overtook his senses.

- As a child, Tesla often described involuntary visions so vivid they appeared externally real, frightening him because he could not distinguish imagination from material reality.

- In the song, this becomes the first dramatic transformation of suffering into genius: what once seemed illness or affliction is revealed as the very mechanism of invention.

- **"What I thought was an affliction turned out to be a gift" is one of the opera's most important identity statements** — Tesla's extraordinary mind is shown not as ordinary intelligence amplified, but as a fundamentally different mode of perception.

- These visions become the foundation of his famous ability to construct inventions completely in his imagination, test them mentally, and perfect them before ever touching tools or materials.

- "Sensing the power of visualization, illuminating flashes were no hallucinations" reframes Tesla's inner visions as cosmic reception rather than delusion — his mind is not malfunctioning, it is tuned to a higher frequency of perception.

- The line "Only a receiver to the great unknown" is central to Tesla's worldview: he often believed he was not inventing in the conventional sense, but receiving truths from a greater universal intelligence already present in nature.

- **"A celestial connection on a cosmic phone" brilliantly captures Tesla's mystical-scientific imagination** — the metaphor suggests he is in direct communication with forces beyond ordinary human reach, receiving transmissions from the universe itself.

- This image elevates Tesla from inventor to intermediary: he becomes the conduit between cosmic intelligence and earthly civilization.

- **"Dream, imagine, create, and wonder are all in the public domain" is a profound democratization of genius** — Tesla is saying that imagination belongs to everyone, not to elites, institutions, or gatekeepers.

- This line reflects Tesla's deepest humanitarian belief: invention is not private ownership of thought, but access to universal creative possibility.

- "An unlimited repertoire plays in my brain" portrays Tesla's mind as an endless symphonic archive of invention — an inexhaustible stream of patterns, mechanisms, and visions continuously unfolding.

- **"Harnessing the sun can't be that tough, I just hadn't thought hard enough" combines wit and grandeur**, showing Tesla's fearless relationship to impossibility: even the sun is merely another engineering problem waiting to be solved.

- **The line expresses Tesla's audacious optimism** — no challenge is inherently impossible, only not yet understood.

- "I can feel the presence of the powers that be, Mount Olympus is contacting me," transforms Tesla into a mythic receiver of divine inspiration.

- Mount Olympus here symbolizes not literal gods descending, but Tesla's sensation that his insights originate from a plane beyond ordinary human reasoning — a realm of archetypal intelligence and cosmic order.

- In the opera's mythology, Tesla becomes the mortal chosen to interpret divine energy into practical form, making him both scientist and priest of light.

- The chorus phrase "Cosmic communications, energy, frequency, and vibrations" directly reflects Tesla's famous philosophical framework — his belief that understanding the universe begins with these three principles.

- These words are not decorative poetry; they are Tesla's scientific cosmology condensed into musical incantation.

- "Power pulsating from pole to pole" evokes Tesla's dream of global electrification — energy flowing freely across the entire earth, connecting humanity into one living network.

- **"Unleashing the world's electrical soul" is one of the opera's grandest metaphors**: electricity is treated not as mechanical utility, but as the hidden spirit of civilization waiting to be awakened.

- **The invocation "Exclaim to Erebus… enough's enough" is one of the most profound symbolic gestures in the entire score.**

- In Greek cosmology, Erebus is not merely darkness, but primordial darkness — the deep pre-creation shadow born from Chaos itself, representing the ancient reign of obscurity and unillumined existence.

- By addressing Erebus directly, Tesla is not fighting mere absence of light, but declaring war on humanity's oldest enemy: ignorance, fear, darkness, and limitation.

- **The phrase means far more than "turn on the lights" — it is a cosmic overthrow of the age of darkness itself.**

- **"From now until forever, let's light it up" becomes the opera's defining proclamation**: Tesla is announcing the permanent triumph of illumination over shadow, knowledge over ignorance, and invention over stagnation.

- This is Tesla's Promethean moment: like the bringer of fire in myth, he is delivering eternal light to humanity and ending the dominion of darkness forever.

- **The bridge — "You can't do that, because it can't be done, the fools would say"** — is Tesla's direct rebuttal to every skeptic, rival, critic, and teacher who ever dismissed his visions as impossible.

- Historically, Tesla encountered constant disbelief from educators, financiers, and peers who lacked the imagination to see what he saw.

- This lyric gives voice to all those early doubters who defined possibility by existing limitations rather than future breakthroughs.

- **"Those who came to scoff would remain to pray"** is a magnificent reversal of judgment: those who mocked him will become witnesses to miracles so astonishing they are reduced from cynicism to reverence.

- The line reveals Tesla's supreme self-confidence — not arrogance, but absolute certainty in the truth of his vision before proof arrives.

- This bridge is also a warning to the world: underestimate Tesla at your own peril, because disbelief is only temporary until reality catches up with imagination.

- Dramatically, "Light It Up" functions as Tesla's declaration of dominion over the opera's central symbolic battlefield — light versus darkness, imagination versus limitation, future versus fear.

- Musically, this song feels expansive, electrifying, and unstoppable — not just a song, but an anthem of awakening, meant to lift the audience into Tesla's own state of visionary exhilaration.

- In the arc of the opera, this number is the clearest statement of Tesla's inner identity: every other song reveals a chapter of his life, but "Light It Up" reveals his essence.

- **The song also unites every major thematic thread in the opera:** prophecy from "Born Tesla," triumph from "Wizard of OZ," cosmic ambition from "Wardenclyffe," and universal service from "Peace."

- It is the anthem because it is Tesla's mission distilled into pure musical form: to receive light from the cosmos, transform it into invention, and give it back to humanity forever.

- "Light It Up" ultimately becomes more than the title of the opera — it is Tesla's command to civilization itself: awaken, illuminate, transcend, and never again surrender the world to darkness.

www.ingramcontent.com/pod-product-compliance
Lightning Source LLC
LaVergne TN
LVHW070150110826
845147LV00002B/366
9798234068514